AMERICAN HISTORY

AMERICAN HISTORY

WALKER DOUGLAS

Interior Illustrations
by Robert Roper

SCHOLASTIC INC.
New York Toronto London Auckland Sydney
Mexico City New Delhi Hong Kong

ISBN 0-439-20211-6

12 11 10 9 8 7 6 5 4 3 2 1   0 1 2 3 4 5/0

Printed in the U.S.A.   01

First Scholastic printing, September 2000

TABLE OF CONTENTS

Introduction   vii
Early Americans   1
Colonial Life   7
Birth of a Nation   14
Slavery and the Civil War   22
The Wild, Wild West   28
Turn of the Century   35
World at War   42
New Frontiers   47

History boring? Well, it certainly doesn't have to be! History can be full of the quirky facts that make life interesting. Bet you didn't know that some early American colonists shaved their heads to make room for the wigs they wore! Well, after you read this book, you will be full of all sorts of fun facts!

This book, however, is meant as a starting ground. What that means is, I hope that when you're finished reading, you'll want to know more about some of the facts presented and do some further investigations. For example, what were the wigs made of? Did they wear them all the time — even to bed? Did men *and* women wear them? It's up to you to get out there and find out! Don't you want to *know it all*?

- The Anasazi Indians lived in houses carved into the sides of cliffs. To get to work in their cornfields each morning, they had to climb hundreds of feet straight up a canyon wall. The Anasazi disappeared without a trace sometime around A.D. 1300.

- Indians of the Northwest Coast would sometimes spend years planning elaborate parties called "potlatches." At these parties, which lasted for days, the host would frequently give away everything he owned.

- By the time Columbus arrived in America, there were already seventy-five million people living here — that's almost one-fourth of the population of the United States today.

- On his fourth voyage to the Americas, Columbus was attacked by Indians but survived because he remembered that a lunar eclipse was about to occur. The Indian chiefs were so impressed by his prediction that they spared Columbus and his men.

- The Spanish brought the horse back to America when they arrived in the fifteenth century. A tiny horselike ancestor had lived in America during the ice age but had become extinct.

- Pocahontas had three names over the course of her life. She was named Matoax ("little snow feather") at birth, then nicknamed Pocahontas ("playful") as a child. She then married John Rolfe and was baptized, under yet another name: Rebecca (from the Hebrew verb, "to bind").

She died in England, of smallpox, at age twenty-two.

- More Native Americans were killed by disease than died in battles. Between 1640 and 1660, the Iroquois Nation lost half of its population to diseases brought by settlers to the New World.

- King James I of England may have been the first public figure to warn of the harmful effects of tobacco. Smoking, he insisted, was "loathsome to the eye, hateful to the nose, harmful to the brain, dangerous to the lungs . . ."

- European women were so rare in the New World that the Virginia Company would actually buy girls from their families to become the wives of settlers in the colonies.

- Although the holds of most seventeenth-century ships stank of garbage, the *Mayflower* is supposed to have had a pleasant smell. The reason? She carried wine barrels, and the barrels leaked.

- Plymouth Rock was not the first place the Pilgrims landed in 1620. By the time they finally stepped onto that famous boulder, they had already landed at several other places on Cape Cod.

- Thanksgiving did not become an official holiday until 1863, when Sarah Josepha Hale, the editor of *Ladies' Magazine*, finally convinced President Lincoln that there ought to be a day to recognize the "Pilgrim" celebration.

- The Pilgrims wore only black on Sundays. The rest of the week they dressed in red or green or blue. Pilgrim children, both boys and girls, wore dresses until they were six years old. After that, the boys dressed like men.

- In Puritan days, you could be fined for running, shaving, or even making your bed on Sundays. Laws forbidding such activities on the Sabbath were called "blue laws," because they were written in books bound in blue paper.

- During the Salem witchcraft trials more than one hundred people were tried as witches. Twenty people and two dogs

were put to death. None were burned. Nineteen people were hanged, and one was crushed by heavy weights.

- Blackbeard the Pirate was finally killed in 1718 in a sea battle off the North Carolina coast. After "five and twenty wounds" he was still fighting for his life when, cocking his pistol for yet another shot, he suddenly fell dead.

- Women in early America "belonged" to their husbands. If a wife ran away, she could be accused of stealing — herself and even her clothing.

- The members of Connecticut's New Haven Colony created their own rules. One rule said that every male had to have his hair "cut round," like an upside-down bowl.

- Johan Printz, the governor of New Sweden (what is today the Delaware Bay region), was the largest man in the colonies. He was seven feet tall and weighed four hundred pounds. The Indians called him "Big Tub." He also introduced the log cabin to America.

GOVERNOR
JOHN "BIG TUB" PRINTZ
BIG MAN,
BIG APPETITE!

AHHHHH...!

YE OLDE
ALL
YOU
CAN
EAT

CLOSED
TILL
FURTHER
NOTICE

- The Dutch settlers of New Amsterdam were the first to bring tulips to the colonies. They also brought stories about a jolly old man named Santa Claus who visited children each year shortly before Christmas, on December 6.

- In designing Philadelphia, William Penn used the idea of a "grid," a pattern of criss-crossing streets. To all the streets going one direction, he assigned numbers; the streets that crossed these he gave names. This same pattern exists today in almost every city in America.

- Benjamin Franklin published a popular almanac (or book of useful facts). In it he also included some wise sayings that are now famous, such as, "A penny saved is a penny earned" and "Three may keep a secret if two of them are dead."

- Benjamin Franklin became a vegetarian at age sixteen. He bought books with the money he saved by not eating meat.

- Benjamin Franklin created many successful inventions, such as bifocal eyeglasses and the lightning rod, but the so-called Franklin stove wasn't one of them. It never worked. The stove that bears his name today was actually invented by a man named Rittenhouse, possibly one of Franklin's friends.

THE DISCOVERY OF ELECTRICITY... –A SHOCKING EXPERIENCE?

DON'T ASK...

- The richest American colonists all wore powdered wigs. Many shaved their heads to make the wigs more comfortable to wear.

- The expression "putting on the dog" came from colonial days, when expensive shoes made from dog hide were considered fashionable.

- Colonial silversmiths sometimes didn't have enough work because wealthy people bought their silverware in England. To make money they made false teeth. The teeth were made of silver.

- Colonial Virginia was a strict Anglican colony. Children could even be taken from their parents if their parents joined the Baptist church.

- In 1770, the New England Quakers became the first organized American group to forbid slavery.

- In 1772, a trip by stagecoach from New York to Boston took six days. Travelers had to wake up at 3 A.M. each morning and ride for eighteen hours a day.

- Today we say that we "ship" a package, even when it travels by truck or plane. That's because in early America nearly all packages traveled by boat.

- Dr. Edward Jenner discovered the smallpox vaccine after he noticed that milkmaids seemed to be immune from the disease. Most people were afraid of the serum he made from cows' blood, but Ben Franklin tried it, and Thomas Jefferson, too. Approximately thirty-six million people died of smallpox during the eighteenth century. That's more than the current population of the entire state of California.

- At the end of the eighteenth century, America was a young country — the average age of its citizens was only sixteen. Today the average age is thirty-three.

- The good ole days weren't exactly the clean ole days. In the late eighteenth century, people dumped their garbage in the street. The pigs and cows were let loose every night to clean up — that is, to eat — some of the mess.

- The first pioneers to explore Vermont had to go on foot rather than on horseback. The trees were so dense there was no grass for a horse to eat.

- The expression "I'm stumped" comes from early pioneer days. Before the first roads were built, hitting a tree stump with

TARNATION! WE'RE STUMPED!

your wagon meant you were stuck, or "stumped," sometimes for several days.

• In Daniel Boone's day, a deerskin was worth a dollar. That's why today we call a dollar a "buck."

- Wish you could drink some history? Well, the brand of tea thrown into Boston Harbor in 1773 can still be bought today from its original makers, Davison Newman of London. The label refers to the Boston Tea Party as a "Grievous Wrong."

- On July 4, 1776, King George of England wrote in his diary, "Nothing of importance happened today." It would be several weeks before news of the signing of the Declaration of Independence reached England by ship.

- Of the three men who rode on the night of April 18, 1773, to warn Patriots that the British were coming, only Samuel Prescott made it to Concord. Paul Revere was captured just west of Lexington, Massachusetts.

- On the day the Revolutionary War began, six British soldiers were so frightened after an ambush that they surrendered to an unarmed woman named Mother Batherick. When they surrendered, she was merely pulling weeds by her pond.

• The song "Yankee Doodle" wasn't written by an American — the British made it up as an insult. But the Patriots said, "Well, then, we'll be Yankee Doodles and proud of it!" and adopted the song as their own.

• After the Revolution, Vermont became its own country, with its own money and its own constitution. It didn't become the fourteenth state until 1791.

- When the patriotic George Washington was asked to serve as the commander in chief of the Continental Army, he agreed on one condition: that he receive no salary.

- American Patriots were the first soldiers in history to actually aim their rifles. Before that, soldiers stood shoulder to shoulder when they fired — and hit whatever happened to be in their way.

- John Hancock's signature was the largest name on the Declaration of Independence. Why? "So the king doesn't have to put on his glasses to read it," he explained.

- Only two people actually signed the Declaration of Independence on July 4, 1776: John Hancock and Charles Thomson. On August 2, it was signed by fifty more delegates. There were still people signing it later that fall.

- Would you believe that George Washington was not the first president of the United States? Contrary to popular belief, there were eight presidents before Washington, beginning with John Hanson of Maryland. Washington was the first president elected under our current Constitution.

- There was no battle fought at Valley Forge during the winter of 1777, even though two thousand soldiers died. Washington's forces suffered from disease and malnutrition, and from the terrible cold.

- Anna-Marie Lane fought alongside her husband in the Revolutionary War disguised as a man. She was never discovered and even received a soldier's pension after the war.

- In 1776, a man named David Bushnell used his newly invented submarine, *Turtle*, to try to sink a British ship. He failed but surprised the British so much that they fled anyway.

- The Revolutionary War lasted for nine years. That's longer than any other war fought by America, except for the war in Vietnam.

- Following the Revolutionary War, New York laid claim to the area that is now the state of Kentucky. They named it Transylvania.

- The first "cowboys" were British sympathizers who used to lure Patriots to their deaths by ringing cowbells. The colonists would follow the sound into the brush thinking there was a lost cow. Then they would be ambushed.

- In 1810, twenty-one-year-old Elijah Fletcher, on a trip to Virginia, wrote home to his family, "I found New Jersey as little inhabited as the wilds of Siberia." Today the population of New Jersey is over eight million.

- The first coin of the official U.S. government came out in 1787. Its motto, suggested by Benjamin Franklin, was "Mind your business."

- John Adams and his wife, Abigail, were the first president and first lady to live in Washington, D.C. At that time, the town was so small they got lost in the woods trying to find it.

- In 1804, Vice President Aaron Burr shot and killed the first treasurer of the United States, Alexander Hamilton, in a duel. Burr was angry because Hamilton had supported Thomas Jefferson instead of him in the presidential election.

- After the War of 1812, the president's house was painted white to hide the burn marks left by the British. That's when everybody began calling it the White House.

- President Thomas Jefferson was so popular that a group from Massachusetts gave him a 1,600-pound cheese as a gift. It arrived in Washington by sleigh in 1801 and was still being eaten four years later at presidential receptions. It was called — you guessed it — "the big cheese."

- Thomas Jefferson and John Adams, two of our Founding Fathers, were the closest of friends, despite their political differences. They died within minutes of each other on July 4, 1826.

- When the Virginia Assembly debated the issue of slavery in 1831, the vote was closer than you might think. Slavery won by less than ten votes.

- Henry "Box" Brown, a slave, had himself packed in a wooden crate and mailed north. When the crate was finally opened in Philadelphia after a twenty-six-hour trip, he asked, "Great God, am I a free man?" After Brown's successful escape was publicized, packages were more heavily inspected.

- Frederick Douglass, an ex-slave whose autobiography taught many people the truth about slavery, had the courage to stand up for his beliefs. Once he was asked to leave a train because he was black, but he wouldn't move. A group of white men had to pull the seat out of the floor of the car to get him off the train.

- John Brown, the leader of the famous antislavery raid on Harpers Ferry, claimed of himself that his stare "could make a cat slink out of the room."

- An escaped slave herself, Harriet Tubman risked her life nineteen times as a "conductor" on the Underground Railroad, carting more than 300 slaves to freedom, including her own elderly parents. She is sometimes called "the black Moses" because she led so many slaves to freedom.

- When the Civil War began, President Lincoln offered the command of the Union Army to Robert E. Lee. Lee refused on the grounds that he could not raise his hand against his home state of Virginia.

- At the beginning of the war, both sides were unprepared for the casualties. After the First Battle of Bull Run, men with bullets in their legs had to walk twenty miles for medical treatment.

- Family rivalries have always existed. Four of Abraham Lincoln's brothers-in-law fought for the South. (Three of them died.) General J.E.B. Stuart of the Confederacy was once pursued on horseback by his own father-in-law, General Cooke of the Union army.

- During the Civil War, Stonewall Jackson was the most feared of all the Southern generals. Up North, mothers told their children to behave "or Stonewall will get you."

- In the South, if you owned twenty or more slaves, you didn't have to fight. In the North, you could buy your way out of the war for about three hundred dollars — a year's wages for most men.

- Abraham Lincoln's son was named Thomas. But he squirmed so much as a child that Lincoln gave him the nickname Tad (short for "tadpole").

SON, THEY SAY IN AMERICA ANYONE CAN GROW UP TO BE PRESIDENT!

- Just before the Battle of Antietam, one of General George McClellan's men discovered three cigars lying on the ground wrapped in a piece of paper. That piece of paper contained General Robert E. Lee's complete plans for the battle.

- Lincoln said that the courage of African-Americans made victory possible for the North. More than 180,000 blacks fought for the Union in the Civil War.

- On the first day of the Battle of Gettysburg — one of the bloodiest battles in U.S. history — some soldiers noticed a wooden sign near a cemetery. The sign warned that anyone firing a gun would be fined five dollars. No fines were ever collected.

- The Union forces lost one quarter of their troops at Gettysburg — that's 23,000 men. The Confederates lost a third of theirs — 28,000 men.

- By the end of the war, Confederate dollar bills were barely worth the paper they were printed on. That's why they were called "shinplasters," because they were only good for bandaging injured legs.

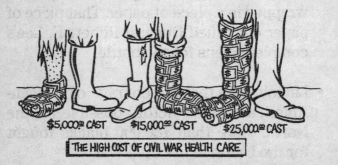

$5,000.00 CAST $15,000.00 CAST $25,000.00 CAST

THE HIGH COST OF CIVIL WAR HEALTH CARE

- According to military tradition, a defeated general was required to surrender his sword. On the day of General Robert E. Lee's surrender, however, General Ulysses S. Grant avoided any mention of that custom, and so Lee left Appomattox with his sword.

- In 1866, the year after the war's end, Mississippi spent one-fifth of its income on artificial arms and legs for war victims.

- Over 600,000 soldiers died during the Civil War. That's almost as many as died in all other U.S. wars put together.

- In 1803, Lewis and Clark left on an expedition to explore the newly purchased Louisiana Territory. It took them more than a year just to cross the Rockies — and they eventually reached the West Coast in 1805. Today, the same journey can be made by plane in less than four hours.

- In 1848, there were 812 people living in San Francisco. Two years later, after gold was found, the population was 25,000.

- The California Gold Rush of 1849 included more than 17,000 Chinese immigrants. Because of discrimination, most weren't allowed to mine for gold.

- Gold was worth sixteen dollars an ounce in 1849. That meant that a hardworking prospector could earn as much as two thousand dollars in one week!

- The Gold Rush created many "ghost towns." When all the gold from an area had been mined, everybody moved on to the next one, leaving their houses and buildings behind.

- Out on the Great Plains it got very cold in winter. Because there were no trees for firewood, settlers had to be creative about keeping warm. So they learned to burn buffalo "chips" (dung) instead.

- Levi Strauss began his career by selling canvas for tents to miners. He only made his fortune, however, when he turned that fabric into the sturdy pants we know today as Levi's jeans.

- It cost a lot of money to stock a covered wagon for the trip out West — as much as fifteen hundred dollars for a large family. That was almost five years' wages for most people!

- Because there were so few stores out West, settlers ordered everything from hats to hay forks from mail-order catalogs. There were even catalogs for ordering brides!

- On the western frontier, boys would sometimes show off for their girlfriends by wrestling pigs. It made the girls laugh, but afterward, said one boy, "We were a mite too muddy to kiss."

- Tombstone, Arizona, was the site of the most famous shoot-out in history: the Gunfight at the OK Corral. But just because it was famous didn't mean it was long. According to eyewitnesses, it was over in thirty seconds.

- While serving as U.S. secretary of war, Jefferson Davis convinced the army to create a "Camel Corps." More than one hundred camels were imported from the Middle East to help soldiers cross the deserts. The camels didn't work out, but they didn't just disappear. Many years later, frontiersmen reported seeing them wandering in the desert.

- On June 22, 1876, Lieutenant Colonel George Armstrong Custer disobeyed orders and attacked the combined forces of the Oglala Sioux Nation. Custer was killed along with all of his men at the Battle of Little Big Horn. The only survivor was a horse called Comanche.

- The great Sioux Indian chief Sitting Bull was originally called "Hunkesni" — a Sioux word that means "slow." One day, after the young Hunkesni had bravely fought in a battle, a lone buffalo came toward his campfire and began to speak. It was the Great Spirit, taking the form of a bull, and he pronounced the young chief's new name — "Tatanka Yotanka," or Sitting Bull.

- Custer is always shown in paintings and photographs sporting long hair. On the day of his death, however, his locks were gone. He'd had his hair cut short the day before.

- William H. Bonney ("Billy the Kid") started gunslinging when he was twelve, but his career lasted less than ten years. He was killed by his former friend, Sheriff Pat Garrett, at the age of twenty-one.

- After the Civil War, Allen Pinkerton started a detective agency that hunted down outlaws like Butch Cassidy and Jesse James. It was the first crime-fighting organization in America to keep files (including photographs) of criminals.

• Not all outlaws in the Wild West were men. There were women, too — like Cattle Annie and Belle Starr, who carried a thousand-dollar bounty on her head.

WANTED

CATTLE ANNIE
$1,000.⁰⁰ REWARD

DON'T LET HER GOOD LOOKS FOOL YOU—SHE'S A KILLER!

- The first coast-to-coast passenger trains advertised that they were "faster and safer" than any other mode of transportation. They went twenty miles per hour, and their crews were supplied with rifles and plenty of ammo in case of attack.

- Actually, the guns were probably a good idea. The trains carried large payrolls and were sometimes robbed. The first American train robbery was in 1866, when the Reno Gang got away with ten thousand dollars in cash.

- The first state to give women the full right to vote was Wyoming, in 1869 — fifty-one years before the Nineteenth Amendment would be passed, giving the vote to the rest of American women.

- When she was a schoolgirl, Susan B. Anthony was told by her teacher that girls only needed to be able to read the Bible and count their "egg money" (grocery money). Instead, Anthony learned mathematics by spying on the boys' math class.

- The game of basketball was invented in Massachusetts in 1891 by Dr. James Naismith. He invented the game to entertain his college students, who complained that they were bored.

- The great steel millionaire Andrew Carnegie spent the last part of his life trying to give away his money. He built concert halls, colleges, and more than three thousand libraries. In all, he gave away 90 percent of his fortune — $324 million.

- No one wanted to publish L. Frank Baum's tale *The Wonderful Wizard of Oz* — they all said it was too silly. Finally, one publisher said he would do it if Baum paid for the printing. The book appeared on August 1, 1900.

- In 1904, Elizabeth Magie of Philadelphia invented The Landlord's Game. It was played on a board with forty spaces — with railroads, utilities, taxes, jail, parking, and rental properties. When the game was patented in 1935, its name had changed to Monopoly.

- No one thought of building skyscrapers until Elisha Graves Otis invented the first safe elevator. Before that most buildings were only five stories tall.

- Ulysses S. Grant, the eighteenth president of the United States, smoked twenty cigars a day. He died of — you guessed it — throat cancer.

- In 1900, the average American worked fifty-nine hours a week for twenty-two cents an hour.

- Guess who are eating their words now! In 1900, the editors of the *Literary Digest* predicted that the horseless carriage (or automobile) would "never come into as common use as the bicycle."

- In 1904, the lowest fare to cross the Atlantic was reduced to ten dollars. In 1907 alone, more than one million immigrants came to the United States.

- In 1907, the Selig Company stopped filming the movie *The Count of Monte Cristo* because it was just too cold in Michigan. The company looked for a warmer place to film and finally settled on Los Angeles, the future home of the motion picture industry.

- In 1913, the Sixteenth Amendment was passed, creating the first U.S. income tax. The average tax payment was forty-one

dollars. Today people can pay thousands of dollars in taxes.

- Today we owe many of our national parks to the fact that Teddy Roosevelt had asthma as a child. His parents sent him to recuperate in the Dakota territories, where he fell in love with the American frontier.

- Teddy Roosevelt expected his commanders to be in good shape. He required each of them to ride a hundred miles on horseback in three days. To show that this was not unreasonable, Roosevelt himself did it in one day.

- When Teddy Roosevelt refused to kill a baby bear while hunting, the word got out. A toy maker in Brooklyn heard about it and made the first "Teddy" bear.

- Teddy Roosevelt allowed his six children to roller-skate in the White House, slide down the banisters, and play hide-and-seek. Sometimes government business had to wait while Roosevelt played tag with them.

- When he was elected president, Woodrow Wilson brought a flock of sheep to keep the White House lawn trimmed. A few years earlier, President Teddy Roosevelt had brought a bear, a badger, a hen, a rabbit, and a pig to trim the lawn.

- President William Howard Taft was so fat that when Yale University offered him a "chair" (professorship) of law, he said no. If they had a "sofa of law," he said, that might work out.

- In 1908, Henry Ford introduced the world's first mass-produced automobile, called the Model T. Six years later he doubled the salary of his production-line workers so that they could each afford to buy one.

- More than nine million men died in World War I. That's more than the entire population of the state of New Jersey today.

- Think knitting is just for girls? Well, during World War I everyone did their part. Schoolboys formed knitting clubs to make clothes for the American troops.

- In a section of the western front, both sides stopped fighting for Christmas. The soldiers gave one another gifts of cigars and jam and even played a game of soccer together.

- World War I was the first time women were formally allowed to serve in the armed forces.

- The smallest spies used during World War I were actually birds. The Allies fitted carrier pigeons with tiny cameras and then dropped them behind enemy lines. And, of course, the birds flew back home.

- The "Spanish" flu epidemic of 1918 was the worst epidemic in recorded history. It killed twenty million people across the world and crippled the war effort on both sides. Back in the United States, in Philadelphia, almost 1,000 people died in a single day.

- In 1928, fifteen nations, including the United States, signed the Kellogg-Briand Pact. The pact basically made war "illegal." However, World War II began just eleven years later.

- Strange fads became popular between the wars. In 1930, Alvin "Shipwreck" Kelly sat on top of a flagpole for forty-nine days. His record has never been broken.

- At the 1933 Olympics in Berlin, Germany, a young African-American athlete named Jesse Owens disproved Adolf Hitler's theory of the German "master race." Owens broke three world records and won four gold medals in the track-and-field events. Hitler left the stadium before the awards ceremony. He refused to stand to honor Owens's achievement.

- During World War II, people donated everything to the military including car bumpers and bacon grease. The car bumpers were used to make planes; the grease was used in explosives.

- During World War II, the U.S. Marines had a secret code that was never broken by the enemy. Why not? The code was developed by Navajo Indians, who based it on their own language, not on English.

- Chips, a husky dog, was awarded the Army's Distinguished Cross for capturing four Italian gunners in Sicily. Later, the War Department took back the medal after deciding that dogs should not be eligible for the award.

- During the war, when fabric was strictly rationed, some women drew "seams" on the backs of their legs to make it look like they were wearing stockings. That was because silk was particularly rare.

- The first computer was invented during World War II. It weighed more than thirty tons and used 18,000 vacuum tubes.

- In 1920, the first year that women were allowed to vote, the women of a small town in Oregon completely took over the town government. Only one-third of the people in Yoncalla were actually women — but they had all voted.

- Radio shows first became popular in the 1920s. Teachers complained that their students stayed up late listening to them and weren't fit for school the following day. Sound familiar?

- In 1925, teacher John Scopes was only twenty-five years old when he was arrested for breaking a Tennessee state law that banned teaching the theory of evolution. Scopes was found guilty, but the decision was later overturned by another judge.

- Before 1926, all movies were silent films with no talking. Words appeared on the bottom of the screen to be read by the audience, and most movie theaters even had a pianist to play the movie's "soundtrack."

- In 1926, the first "talkie" motion picture, *Don Juan*, was released. It starred Drew Barrymore's great-grandfather, John.

- In 1922, girls in skirtless bathing suits were "measured" by policemen to see how much leg they were showing. Those who were showing too much got arrested for "indecent exposure."

- By 1927, there were already twenty-one million automobiles in America. Shortly afterward, the first highway "cloverleaf" appeared in Woodbridge, New Jersey. Its purpose was to prevent traffic jams.

- The Empire State Building was erected in 1931. With 102 stories, 73 elevators, and 11,860 steps, it was the tallest building in the world.

- On the night of October 30, 1938, a young actor named Orson Welles threw the citizens of the United States into a panic. He broadcast a radio version of H.G. Wells's sci-fi thriller *The War of the Worlds* as if it were a real news story. More than one million people said they believed that Martians had invaded New Jersey.

- In 1948, two brothers opened the world's first fast-food restaurant. Their names were Maurice and Richard McDonald.

- On February 29, 1956, an African-American woman named Rosa Parks sat in the whites-only section of a Montgomery, Alabama, city bus. She refused to leave and was arrested. Her story convinced many people to join the civil rights movement.

- Barbie, the first fashion model doll, appeared in toy stores in 1959. She came with a complete wardrobe and cost only three dollars. More than 350,000 were sold that year.

- In 1960, Vice President Richard M. Nixon and Massachusetts senator John F. Kennedy participated in the first televised presidential debate. Most people thought Kennedy looked comfortable on camera while Nixon did not — and, of course, Kennedy later won the election.

- By 1963, "Beatlemania" had gotten so bad that fans could no longer hear the music at Beatles concerts. There were too many screaming girls.

- When astronaut Neil Armstrong first set foot on the moon in 1969, his words were actually, "One small step for a man, one giant leap for mankind." Because of poor reception, the word *a* was never heard.

- That same year, nearly a half million people attended the Woodstock Music and Arts Festival, the largest festival of the "hippie generation." Strangely enough, the concert wasn't actually held in Woodstock, New York, but on a farm some fifty miles away.

- The first Apple computer appeared in 1977, the first IBM personal computer in 1981. In 1991, nearly every business in America would have computers.

- The first pocket calculators appeared in the 1970s. Their price was around 150 dollars. Today the same calculators can be bought for as little as three or four dollars.